50 International Rice Dishes for Home

By: Kelly Johnson

Table of Contents

- Paella (Spain)
- Biryani (India)
- Risotto (Italy)
- Jollof Rice (West Africa)
- Sushi Rice (Japan)
- Fried Rice (China)
- Arroz con Pollo (Latin America)
- Pilaf (Turkey)
- Dolma (Middle East)
- Nasi Lemak (Malaysia)
- Congee (China)
- Arroz Caldoso (Spain)
- Maki Rolls (Japan)
- Hainanese Chicken Rice (Singapore)
- Tabbouleh (Lebanon)
- Kibbeh (Lebanon)
- Mango Sticky Rice (Thailand)
- Zafrani Pulao (India)
- Rice Pudding (Various Cultures)
- Khao Pad (Thailand)
- Fesenjan (Iran)
- Saffron Rice (Iran)
- Loco Moco (Hawaii)
- Koshari (Egypt)
- Pilau Rice (East Africa)
- Basmati Rice with Curry (India)
- Gallo Pinto (Costa Rica)
- Puto (Philippines)
- Tteokbokki Rice Cake (Korea)
- Mofongo (Puerto Rico)
- Arroz de Marisco (Portugal)
- Fried Rice with Shrimp (China)
- Nasi Goreng (Indonesia)
- Cabbage and Rice (Eastern Europe)
- Risotto al Nero di Seppia (Italy)

- Stuffed Peppers with Rice (Mediterranean)
- Grilled Rice (Japan)
- Red Beans and Rice (USA)
- Roasted Rice (Thailand)
- Chahan (Japan)
- Leblebi Pilavi (Turkey)
- Rice with Beans (Brazil)
- Koshari (Egypt)
- Lentejas con Arroz (Spain)
- Aborrajados Rice (Colombia)
- Spicy Rice with Chicken (Mexico)
- Stuffed Grape Leaves with Rice (Middle East)
- Sticky Rice with Pork (Laos)
- Grits and Rice (USA)
- Savory Rice with Pork (Latin America)

Paella (Spain)

Ingredients:

- 2 tbsp olive oil
- 1 onion, chopped
- 1 red bell pepper, chopped
- 2 garlic cloves, minced
- 1 1/2 cups Arborio rice
- 1/2 tsp saffron threads (optional)
- 4 cups chicken or seafood broth
- 1/2 lb chicken thighs, cut into pieces
- 1/2 lb shrimp, peeled and deveined
- 1/2 lb mussels or clams
- 1/2 lb chorizo, sliced
- 1 cup peas
- 1 lemon, cut into wedges
- Salt and pepper to taste
- Fresh parsley for garnish

Instructions:

1. In a large pan, heat olive oil over medium heat. Add onion, bell pepper, and garlic, and sauté for 5-7 minutes until softened.
2. Stir in rice and saffron (if using), and cook for 2 minutes, letting the rice absorb the flavors.
3. Add the broth, chicken, shrimp, mussels, chorizo, peas, salt, and pepper. Bring to a boil, then reduce heat to low.
4. Cover and simmer for 20-25 minutes, until the rice is tender and the liquid is absorbed.
5. Garnish with lemon wedges and fresh parsley before serving.

Biryani (India)

Ingredients:

- 2 tbsp ghee or vegetable oil
- 1 onion, thinly sliced
- 2 garlic cloves, minced
- 1 tbsp grated ginger
- 1 1/2 cups basmati rice
- 3 cups chicken or vegetable broth
- 1/2 lb chicken, lamb, or vegetables (your choice), cut into pieces
- 1 tsp ground cumin
- 1 tsp ground coriander
- 1 tsp turmeric
- 1/2 tsp ground cinnamon
- 1/2 tsp ground cardamom
- 1/2 tsp ground cloves
- 1 bay leaf
- Salt to taste
- 1/4 cup yogurt (optional)
- Fresh cilantro for garnish
- Fried onions for garnish (optional)

Instructions:

1. In a large pot, heat ghee over medium heat. Add onion and sauté for 5 minutes until golden brown.
2. Stir in garlic, ginger, and spices (cumin, coriander, turmeric, cinnamon, cardamom, and cloves). Cook for 1-2 minutes until fragrant.
3. Add the rice and toast it for 2 minutes, then pour in the broth and bring to a boil.
4. Add the chicken or lamb, bay leaf, and salt. Cover and reduce heat to low. Simmer for 20-25 minutes, until the rice is cooked and the liquid is absorbed.
5. If using, stir in yogurt for added creaminess. Garnish with cilantro and fried onions.

Risotto (Italy)

Ingredients:

- 2 tbsp butter
- 1 onion, chopped
- 1 1/2 cups Arborio rice
- 1/2 cup dry white wine
- 4 cups chicken or vegetable broth, warmed
- 1/2 cup grated Parmesan cheese
- 1 tbsp olive oil
- Salt and pepper to taste

Instructions:

1. In a large saucepan, melt butter with olive oil over medium heat. Add onion and cook for 5-7 minutes until softened.
2. Add the Arborio rice and cook, stirring constantly, for 2-3 minutes until the rice is lightly toasted.
3. Pour in the white wine and cook, stirring, until it is absorbed.
4. Gradually add the warm broth, one ladle at a time, stirring frequently. Allow each addition to be absorbed before adding more.
5. Continue until the rice is tender and creamy, about 18-20 minutes. Stir in Parmesan cheese and season with salt and pepper.

Jollof Rice (West Africa)

Ingredients:

- 2 tbsp vegetable oil
- 1 onion, chopped
- 1 bell pepper, chopped
- 2 tomatoes, blended or chopped
- 1 tbsp tomato paste
- 1/2 tsp ground cumin
- 1/2 tsp ground coriander
- 1 tsp thyme
- 2 cups long-grain rice
- 4 cups chicken or vegetable broth
- 1 tbsp hot sauce (optional)
- Salt and pepper to taste
- Fresh parsley for garnish

Instructions:

1. Heat vegetable oil in a large pot over medium heat. Add onion and bell pepper, and sauté for 5-7 minutes until softened.
2. Stir in the tomatoes, tomato paste, cumin, coriander, and thyme. Cook for 5 minutes, allowing the tomato paste to caramelize slightly.
3. Add the rice, broth, hot sauce (if using), salt, and pepper. Bring to a boil, then reduce heat to low.
4. Cover and simmer for 20-25 minutes, until the rice is cooked and the liquid is absorbed. Fluff with a fork and garnish with fresh parsley.

Sushi Rice (Japan)

Ingredients:

- 2 cups sushi rice
- 2 1/2 cups water
- 1/4 cup rice vinegar
- 2 tbsp sugar
- 1 tsp salt

Instructions:

1. Rinse the sushi rice under cold water until the water runs clear. Drain well.
2. In a pot, combine rice and water. Bring to a boil, then cover and reduce heat to low. Simmer for 18-20 minutes, then remove from heat and let it sit, covered, for 10 minutes.
3. In a small bowl, combine rice vinegar, sugar, and salt. Heat gently to dissolve the sugar.
4. Once the rice has cooled slightly, drizzle the vinegar mixture over the rice and gently fold it in. Let the rice cool to room temperature before using for sushi.

Fried Rice (China)

Ingredients:

- 2 tbsp vegetable oil
- 2 eggs, beaten
- 1 onion, chopped
- 1 cup cooked rice (preferably day-old)
- 1 cup mixed vegetables (peas, carrots, corn)
- 2 garlic cloves, minced
- 3 tbsp soy sauce
- 1/2 tsp sesame oil
- Salt and pepper to taste
- Green onions for garnish

Instructions:

1. Heat vegetable oil in a large pan or wok over medium heat. Add eggs and scramble until cooked through. Remove from the pan and set aside.
2. Add more oil to the pan and sauté onion and garlic for 2-3 minutes.
3. Stir in the cooked rice, mixed vegetables, soy sauce, and sesame oil. Stir-fry for 5-7 minutes until the rice is heated through and slightly crispy.
4. Add the scrambled eggs back to the pan, season with salt and pepper, and garnish with green onions.

Arroz con Pollo (Latin America)

Ingredients:

- 2 tbsp olive oil
- 4 bone-in chicken thighs
- 1 onion, chopped
- 2 garlic cloves, minced
- 1 red bell pepper, chopped
- 2 cups long-grain rice
- 3 cups chicken broth
- 1 can (14 oz) diced tomatoes
- 1 tsp ground cumin
- 1 tsp ground paprika
- 1/2 tsp ground turmeric
- Salt and pepper to taste
- Fresh cilantro for garnish

Instructions:

1. Heat olive oil in a large pot over medium heat. Season chicken with salt and pepper, and brown on both sides, about 5 minutes per side. Remove from the pot and set aside.
2. Add onion, garlic, and bell pepper to the pot, and sauté for 5 minutes.
3. Stir in rice, broth, tomatoes, cumin, paprika, turmeric, and the browned chicken. Bring to a boil, then cover and reduce heat to low.
4. Simmer for 20-25 minutes, until the rice is cooked and the chicken is tender. Garnish with fresh cilantro.

Pilaf (Turkey)

Ingredients:

- 2 tbsp butter or olive oil
- 1 onion, chopped
- 1 cup long-grain rice
- 2 cups chicken or vegetable broth
- 1/4 cup toasted pine nuts
- 1/4 cup dried currants or raisins
- 1/2 tsp ground cinnamon
- Salt and pepper to taste
- Fresh parsley for garnish

Instructions:

1. In a large pot, heat butter or oil over medium heat. Add onion and sauté for 5 minutes.
2. Stir in rice and cook for 2-3 minutes, until lightly toasted.
3. Add broth, pine nuts, currants, cinnamon, salt, and pepper. Bring to a boil, then cover and reduce heat to low.
4. Simmer for 18-20 minutes, until the rice is tender and the liquid is absorbed.
5. Fluff the rice with a fork and garnish with fresh parsley before serving.

Dolma (Middle East)

Ingredients:

- 1 cup long-grain rice
- 1/2 lb ground lamb or beef
- 1 onion, finely chopped
- 2 tbsp olive oil
- 1 tbsp pine nuts
- 1/2 tsp cinnamon
- 1/2 tsp allspice
- 1/4 cup fresh dill, chopped
- 1/4 cup fresh parsley, chopped
- 1 tbsp lemon juice
- 1 jar grape leaves, rinsed
- Salt and pepper to taste
- 2 cups vegetable broth

Instructions:

1. In a pan, heat olive oil and sauté onion until translucent. Add ground meat and cook until browned.
2. Stir in rice, pine nuts, cinnamon, allspice, dill, parsley, lemon juice, salt, and pepper. Remove from heat and let it cool.
3. Lay grape leaves flat and place a spoonful of filling in the center. Roll tightly, folding in the sides.
4. Arrange the dolmas in a pot, layering them tightly. Add vegetable broth to cover, and simmer for 30-40 minutes, until rice is tender.

Nasi Lemak (Malaysia)

Ingredients:

- 1 1/2 cups jasmine rice
- 1 1/2 cups coconut milk
- 1 cup water
- 1 pandan leaf (optional)
- 1/2 tsp salt
- 1/2 lb fried anchovies (ikan bilis)
- 2 hard-boiled eggs, halved
- 1 cucumber, sliced
- 1/2 cup sambal (spicy chili paste)
- 1 tbsp fried peanuts

Instructions:

1. Rinse the rice under cold water until clear. In a pot, combine rice, coconut milk, water, pandan leaf, and salt. Cook until rice is tender and fragrant, about 20 minutes.
2. Serve the rice with fried anchovies, hard-boiled eggs, cucumber slices, sambal, and fried peanuts for garnish.

Congee (China)

Ingredients:

- 1 cup jasmine rice
- 8 cups chicken or vegetable broth
- 1/2 lb chicken breast or pork, thinly sliced (optional)
- 2 slices ginger
- 2 tbsp soy sauce
- 1/2 tsp sesame oil
- 2 green onions, sliced
- 1 boiled egg, sliced (optional)
- Salt to taste

Instructions:

1. In a large pot, combine rice and broth. Bring to a boil, then reduce to a simmer. Cook for 1-1.5 hours, stirring occasionally, until the rice breaks down and the congee reaches a porridge-like consistency.
2. Add meat, ginger, soy sauce, and sesame oil, and simmer for another 10 minutes.
3. Serve hot with green onions, boiled egg slices, and a dash of soy sauce.

Arroz Caldoso (Spain)

Ingredients:

- 1 cup short-grain rice
- 2 tbsp olive oil
- 1 onion, chopped
- 2 garlic cloves, minced
- 1 red bell pepper, chopped
- 2 tomatoes, chopped
- 4 cups chicken or seafood broth
- 1/2 lb seafood (shrimp, mussels, clams, or fish)
- 1/2 tsp smoked paprika
- Saffron threads (optional)
- Fresh parsley, chopped
- Lemon wedges

Instructions:

1. In a large pot, heat olive oil over medium heat. Add onion, garlic, and bell pepper. Sauté until soft, about 5 minutes.
2. Stir in tomatoes and cook for another 3 minutes until softened. Add rice, paprika, and saffron (if using).
3. Pour in the broth and bring to a boil. Reduce heat and simmer for 15-20 minutes.
4. Add seafood, cook for another 5-7 minutes until the seafood is cooked. Garnish with parsley and serve with lemon wedges.

Maki Rolls (Japan)

Ingredients:

- 2 cups sushi rice
- 2 1/2 cups water
- 1/4 cup rice vinegar
- 2 tbsp sugar
- 1/2 tsp salt
- 5-6 sheets nori (seaweed)
- 1 cucumber, julienned
- 1 avocado, sliced
- 1/2 lb sushi-grade tuna or salmon, sliced
- Soy sauce and wasabi for serving

Instructions:

1. Rinse rice under cold water until the water runs clear. Cook the rice with water according to the package instructions.
2. In a small bowl, combine vinegar, sugar, and salt. Heat gently until dissolved. Stir into cooked rice and cool.
3. Place a sheet of nori on a bamboo sushi mat. Spread a thin layer of rice over the nori, leaving a small border at the top.
4. Place fillings (cucumber, avocado, fish) in the center. Roll tightly, pressing the edges to seal.
5. Slice the roll into bite-sized pieces and serve with soy sauce and wasabi.

Hainanese Chicken Rice (Singapore)

Ingredients:

- 1 whole chicken (about 3-4 lbs)
- 5 cups jasmine rice
- 1 tbsp vegetable oil
- 4 garlic cloves, minced
- 2 tbsp ginger, minced
- 2 tbsp soy sauce
- 2 tbsp sesame oil
- Salt to taste
- Fresh cucumber, sliced
- Chili sauce (optional)

Instructions:

1. Boil the chicken in a large pot of water for 45-60 minutes, until fully cooked. Remove the chicken and set aside. Reserve the broth.
2. Heat vegetable oil in a pan, sauté garlic and ginger until fragrant. Add rice and stir for 2-3 minutes.
3. Add 5 cups of the chicken broth and cook rice until tender (about 15-20 minutes).
4. Serve the chicken, rice, cucumber slices, and a side of chili sauce for dipping.

Tabbouleh (Lebanon)

Ingredients:

- 1 cup bulgur wheat
- 2 cups hot water
- 1/2 cup fresh parsley, chopped
- 1/2 cup fresh mint, chopped
- 2 tomatoes, diced
- 1 cucumber, diced
- 1/4 cup olive oil
- 2 tbsp lemon juice
- Salt and pepper to taste

Instructions:

1. Place the bulgur in a bowl, cover with hot water, and let it soak for 15 minutes. Drain any excess water.
2. In a large bowl, combine the bulgur, parsley, mint, tomatoes, and cucumber.
3. Drizzle with olive oil and lemon juice. Season with salt and pepper to taste. Toss and serve chilled.

Kibbeh (Lebanon)

Ingredients:

- 1 lb ground lamb or beef
- 1 1/2 cups fine bulgur wheat
- 1 onion, chopped
- 1/2 cup pine nuts, toasted
- 1 tsp cinnamon
- 1 tsp allspice
- Salt and pepper to taste
- Olive oil for frying

Instructions:

1. Soak the bulgur in warm water for 15-20 minutes, then drain and squeeze out excess water.
2. Combine the meat, bulgur, onion, spices, and salt in a bowl. Mix until well combined.
3. For filling, sauté onions and pine nuts in olive oil. Stir in cooked meat and season.
4. Shape the kibbeh mixture into ovals, stuffing them with the filling. Fry in hot oil until golden and crispy.

Mango Sticky Rice (Thailand)

Ingredients:

- 1 cup glutinous rice
- 1 1/4 cups coconut milk
- 1/4 cup sugar
- 1/4 tsp salt
- 2 ripe mangoes, peeled and sliced

Instructions:

1. Rinse the rice under cold water until the water runs clear. Steam the rice for 20-25 minutes until tender.
2. In a saucepan, combine coconut milk, sugar, and salt. Heat until sugar dissolves.
3. Stir the coconut milk mixture into the cooked rice. Let it absorb and cool to room temperature.
4. Serve the sticky rice with fresh mango slices.

Zafrani Pulao (India)

Ingredients:

- 1 1/2 cups basmati rice
- 2 tbsp ghee (clarified butter)
- 1 large onion, thinly sliced
- 1/2 tsp cumin seeds
- 4-5 cardamom pods
- 1 cinnamon stick
- 1 bay leaf
- 1/4 tsp saffron threads
- 1/2 cup warm milk
- 1/4 cup raisins
- 1/4 cup cashews, chopped
- Salt to taste
- 3 cups water

Instructions:

1. Soak the saffron threads in warm milk and set aside.
2. Rinse the rice thoroughly and soak for 20 minutes, then drain.
3. Heat ghee in a pot, and sauté cumin seeds, cardamom, cinnamon, and bay leaf until fragrant.
4. Add the sliced onion and cook until golden. Add the rice and sauté for 2-3 minutes.
5. Add water, saffron milk, raisins, cashews, and salt. Bring to a boil, then cover and simmer for 15-20 minutes until rice is tender and water is absorbed. Fluff the rice with a fork and serve.

Rice Pudding (Various Cultures)

Ingredients:

- 1 cup white rice (short or medium grain)
- 4 cups milk (or dairy-free milk alternative)
- 1/2 cup sugar
- 1/2 tsp vanilla extract
- 1/4 tsp ground cinnamon (optional)
- Pinch of salt
- Raisins or other dried fruit (optional)

Instructions:

1. Rinse the rice under cold water. In a medium saucepan, combine the rice, milk, sugar, vanilla, cinnamon, and salt.
2. Bring the mixture to a boil, then reduce heat to low and simmer, stirring occasionally for 30-40 minutes, until the rice is tender and the mixture thickens.
3. Remove from heat and let it cool. Serve warm or chilled, garnished with raisins or other dried fruit if desired.

Khao Pad (Thailand)

Ingredients:

- 3 cups cooked jasmine rice (preferably cold)
- 2 tbsp vegetable oil
- 1/2 onion, diced
- 2 garlic cloves, minced
- 1/2 cup mixed vegetables (peas, carrots, corn)
- 2 eggs, lightly beaten
- 1 tbsp soy sauce
- 1 tbsp fish sauce
- 1 tbsp sugar
- 1/2 tsp white pepper
- Fresh cilantro, chopped
- Lime wedges, for serving

Instructions:

1. Heat vegetable oil in a wok or large pan over medium heat. Sauté the onion and garlic until fragrant.
2. Add the mixed vegetables and cook for 2-3 minutes until tender.
3. Push the vegetables to the side and pour in the beaten eggs. Scramble the eggs until cooked through.
4. Add the rice to the pan, breaking up any clumps. Stir in soy sauce, fish sauce, sugar, and pepper.
5. Cook, stirring for another 5 minutes, allowing the rice to fry. Garnish with cilantro and serve with lime wedges.

Fesenjan (Iran)

Ingredients:

- 2 chicken breasts or thighs
- 1 large onion, finely chopped
- 2 tbsp vegetable oil
- 1/2 tsp turmeric
- 1/2 tsp cinnamon
- 1/2 tsp ground ginger
- 1/2 tsp cumin
- 2 cups pomegranate juice
- 1/2 cup ground walnuts
- 2 tbsp sugar (optional, depending on sweetness of pomegranate juice)
- Salt and pepper to taste
- Fresh parsley, for garnish

Instructions:

1. Heat oil in a large pan. Add the onions and sauté until golden.
2. Add the chicken and brown on both sides. Stir in the turmeric, cinnamon, ginger, and cumin, and cook for 2 minutes.
3. Pour in the pomegranate juice, ground walnuts, and sugar. Bring to a simmer, cover, and cook for 40-45 minutes, until the chicken is tender and the sauce has thickened.
4. Adjust salt and pepper to taste, and garnish with fresh parsley before serving.

Saffron Rice (Iran)

Ingredients:

- 2 cups basmati rice
- 1/4 tsp saffron threads
- 3 tbsp hot water
- 2 tbsp butter or ghee
- 1 onion, finely chopped
- 1/2 tsp cumin seeds
- 3 cups water
- Salt to taste

Instructions:

1. Soak the saffron threads in 3 tbsp hot water and set aside.
2. Rinse the rice under cold water and soak for 30 minutes. Drain the rice.
3. Heat butter or ghee in a large pot. Add cumin seeds and onion, sautéing until golden brown.
4. Add the rice to the pot, followed by water and salt. Bring to a boil, then reduce the heat and cover. Simmer for 15-20 minutes until the rice is cooked.
5. Drizzle the saffron water over the rice and fluff gently before serving.

Loco Moco (Hawaii)

Ingredients:

- 2 cups cooked rice (white or brown)
- 2 hamburger patties
- 1/4 cup beef gravy
- 2 eggs, fried sunny-side up
- Salt and pepper to taste
- Green onions for garnish (optional)

Instructions:

1. Cook the hamburger patties to your desired doneness and season with salt and pepper.
2. In a separate pan, fry the eggs sunny-side up.
3. Place the cooked rice in bowls, top with a hamburger patty, and pour beef gravy over the patty.
4. Add a fried egg on top of each bowl and garnish with green onions.

Koshari (Egypt)

Ingredients:

- 1 cup lentils
- 1 1/2 cups short-grain rice
- 1/2 cup macaroni or pasta (optional)
- 1 onion, thinly sliced
- 2 tbsp vegetable oil
- 2 cups tomato sauce
- 2 garlic cloves, minced
- 1 tsp ground cumin
- Salt and pepper to taste
- Crispy fried onions (optional)

Instructions:

1. Cook the lentils in boiling water for 15-20 minutes, until tender. Drain and set aside.
2. Cook the rice according to package instructions.
3. Cook the pasta in salted water and drain.
4. In a large pan, heat oil and sauté the onion until golden and crispy. Remove and set aside.
5. In the same pan, add garlic, cumin, and tomato sauce, cooking for 5 minutes. Season with salt and pepper.
6. To serve, layer the rice, lentils, and pasta, then top with the tomato sauce and crispy onions.

Pilau Rice (East Africa)

Ingredients:

- 2 cups basmati rice
- 1 onion, chopped
- 2 garlic cloves, minced
- 1 tsp ground cumin
- 1/2 tsp ground cinnamon
- 1/2 tsp turmeric
- 1 tbsp vegetable oil
- 3 cups water or vegetable broth
- Salt to taste
- Fresh cilantro for garnish

Instructions:

1. Rinse the rice under cold water and drain.
2. Heat oil in a pot over medium heat. Add onion and garlic, sautéing until soft.
3. Stir in the cumin, cinnamon, and turmeric, cooking for 1-2 minutes.
4. Add the rice and water or broth. Bring to a boil, then reduce heat and simmer for 15-20 minutes, until the rice is tender.
5. Fluff the rice with a fork and garnish with fresh cilantro before serving.

Basmati Rice with Curry (India)

Ingredients:

- 2 cups basmati rice
- 1 onion, chopped
- 2 garlic cloves, minced
- 1-inch piece ginger, grated
- 1 tbsp curry powder
- 1/2 tsp turmeric
- 1/2 tsp cumin
- 1/2 tsp garam masala
- 3 cups water
- 2 tbsp ghee or vegetable oil
- Salt to taste
- Fresh cilantro, for garnish

Instructions:

1. Rinse the basmati rice under cold water until the water runs clear. Soak the rice for 15-20 minutes and then drain.
2. Heat ghee or oil in a large saucepan. Add the chopped onion and cook until golden.
3. Add the garlic and ginger, and cook for another 1-2 minutes.
4. Stir in the curry powder, turmeric, cumin, and garam masala. Cook for 1-2 minutes to release the spices' aroma.
5. Add the soaked rice to the pan and sauté for a couple of minutes.
6. Pour in the water and season with salt. Bring to a boil, then reduce the heat, cover, and simmer for 15-20 minutes, until the rice is tender and the water is absorbed.
7. Fluff the rice with a fork and garnish with fresh cilantro before serving.

Gallo Pinto (Costa Rica)

Ingredients:

- 2 cups cooked white rice (preferably cold)
- 1 cup cooked black beans (or canned black beans, drained and rinsed)
- 1 small onion, chopped
- 1 red bell pepper, chopped
- 2 garlic cloves, minced
- 2 tbsp vegetable oil
- 1/4 cup fresh cilantro, chopped
- 2 tbsp salsa Lizano (optional but traditional)
- Salt and pepper to taste

Instructions:

1. Heat oil in a large skillet over medium heat. Add the onion, red bell pepper, and garlic, cooking until the vegetables soften, about 5 minutes.
2. Stir in the black beans and cook for another 2-3 minutes.
3. Add the cold cooked rice and salsa Lizano (if using). Stir everything together, breaking up any clumps of rice.
4. Cook, stirring occasionally, for 5-7 minutes until everything is heated through and well mixed.
5. Season with salt and pepper to taste, and stir in fresh cilantro before serving.

Puto (Philippines)

Ingredients:

- 2 cups rice flour
- 1 cup coconut milk
- 1/2 cup sugar
- 2 tsp baking powder
- 1/2 tsp salt
- 1/2 cup water
- 1 tsp vanilla extract
- 10-12 slices cheese (optional, for topping)

Instructions:

1. In a large mixing bowl, combine rice flour, sugar, baking powder, and salt.
2. Add the coconut milk, water, and vanilla extract. Mix well until a smooth batter forms.
3. Grease small molds or cupcake liners and pour the batter into each mold, filling about 2/3 full.
4. If using cheese, place a slice on top of each batter-filled mold.
5. Steam the puto in a steamer for 20-25 minutes, or until a toothpick inserted comes out clean.
6. Remove from the steamer and let cool before serving.

Tteokbokki Rice Cake (Korea)

Ingredients:

- 1 pound Korean rice cakes (tteok)
- 1 tbsp vegetable oil
- 1 small onion, thinly sliced
- 2 garlic cloves, minced
- 2 tbsp gochujang (Korean chili paste)
- 1 tbsp soy sauce
- 1 tbsp sugar
- 2 cups water or dashi (broth)
- 1 hard-boiled egg (optional, for serving)
- Sesame seeds, for garnish
- Green onions, chopped, for garnish

Instructions:

1. Soak the rice cakes in warm water for 20-30 minutes if they are dry.
2. Heat oil in a pan over medium heat. Add the onion and garlic, and sauté for 3-4 minutes until softened.
3. Stir in the gochujang, soy sauce, and sugar. Cook for 1-2 minutes until the paste is fragrant.
4. Add the water or dashi, bringing the mixture to a simmer.
5. Add the soaked rice cakes to the pan and cook for 10-15 minutes, stirring occasionally, until the sauce thickens and the rice cakes are soft.
6. Garnish with chopped green onions, sesame seeds, and a hard-boiled egg if desired. Serve warm.

Mofongo (Puerto Rico)

Ingredients:

- 2 large green plantains, peeled and sliced
- 2 tbsp olive oil
- 4 garlic cloves, minced
- 1/2 cup pork cracklings (chicharrones) or bacon bits
- Salt to taste
- 1/4 cup chicken broth (optional)

Instructions:

1. In a large pan, heat oil over medium heat and fry the sliced plantains in batches until golden and tender, about 4-5 minutes per batch.
2. Remove the fried plantains and drain on paper towels.
3. In a mortar and pestle, mash the garlic with a pinch of salt. Add the fried plantains and pork cracklings (or bacon), and mash them together until combined. If needed, add chicken broth for moisture.
4. Serve the mofongo as a side dish or top with your choice of meat or seafood.

Arroz de Marisco (Portugal)

Ingredients:

- 1 1/2 cups short-grain rice
- 1 lb mixed seafood (shrimp, clams, mussels, squid)
- 1 onion, chopped
- 2 garlic cloves, minced
- 1 bell pepper, chopped
- 1 tomato, chopped
- 2 tbsp olive oil
- 4 cups fish or vegetable stock
- 1/2 cup white wine
- 1 tsp paprika
- 1/2 tsp saffron (optional)
- Salt and pepper to taste
- Fresh parsley, chopped, for garnish

Instructions:

1. Heat olive oil in a large pot. Sauté onion, garlic, and bell pepper until softened.
2. Add chopped tomato, paprika, and saffron (if using), and cook for another 3 minutes.
3. Stir in the rice, cooking for 2-3 minutes, then add the white wine and let it cook off.
4. Pour in the stock and bring to a simmer. Cook the rice uncovered for 15-20 minutes, adding more stock if needed.
5. Add the seafood, and cook for an additional 10 minutes, until the seafood is cooked through and the rice is tender.
6. Season with salt and pepper, garnish with parsley, and serve hot.

Fried Rice with Shrimp (China)

Ingredients:

- 2 cups cold cooked rice (preferably day-old rice)
- 1/2 lb shrimp, peeled and deveined
- 1 onion, chopped
- 2 garlic cloves, minced
- 1/2 cup peas and carrots (frozen or fresh)
- 2 eggs, beaten
- 3 tbsp soy sauce
- 1 tbsp sesame oil
- 1 tbsp vegetable oil
- Green onions for garnish

Instructions:

1. Heat the vegetable oil in a wok or large skillet over medium-high heat. Add the shrimp and cook until pink, about 2-3 minutes. Remove and set aside.
2. In the same pan, add a bit more oil and sauté the onion, garlic, and peas/carrots for 3-4 minutes.
3. Push the veggies to one side of the pan, and scramble the eggs on the other side.
4. Add the rice, soy sauce, and sesame oil, stirring to combine. Add the shrimp back into the pan and mix well.
5. Cook for another 3-4 minutes, ensuring everything is heated through.
6. Garnish with chopped green onions and serve.

Nasi Goreng (Indonesia)

Ingredients:

- 2 cups cold cooked rice
- 2 tbsp vegetable oil
- 1 onion, chopped
- 2 garlic cloves, minced
- 2 eggs, scrambled
- 1/2 cup cooked chicken, chopped (optional)
- 1/2 cup cooked shrimp (optional)
- 1 tbsp soy sauce
- 1 tbsp sweet soy sauce (kecap manis)
- 1 tsp chili paste (optional, for spice)
- 1/4 cup green onions, chopped
- Cucumber slices, for garnish

Instructions:

1. Heat vegetable oil in a large pan or wok over medium heat. Add the onion and garlic, and cook for 3-4 minutes.
2. Push the onions and garlic to the side, and scramble the eggs in the same pan.
3. Add the cold rice, soy sauce, sweet soy sauce, and chili paste (if using), and stir-fry for 5-7 minutes until heated through.
4. Stir in the cooked chicken and shrimp, and cook for another 2-3 minutes.
5. Garnish with chopped green onions and serve with cucumber slices.

Cabbage and Rice (Eastern Europe)

Ingredients:

- 2 cups cooked rice
- 1 small cabbage, chopped
- 1 onion, chopped
- 2 tbsp vegetable oil
- 1/2 tsp caraway seeds
- Salt and pepper to taste
- 1/4 cup sour cream (optional)

Instructions:

1. Heat oil in a large skillet over medium heat. Add the chopped onion and sauté until softened.
2. Stir in the caraway seeds and chopped cabbage, and cook for 10-12 minutes, stirring occasionally, until the cabbage wilts and begins to brown.
3. Add the cooked rice and stir to combine. Cook for an additional 5 minutes, allowing the flavors to meld together.
4. Season with salt and pepper to taste. Optionally, top with a dollop of sour cream before serving.

Risotto al Nero di Seppia (Italy)

Ingredients:

- 1 1/2 cups Arborio rice
- 2 tbsp olive oil
- 1 small onion, chopped
- 2 garlic cloves, minced
- 1/2 cup dry white wine
- 4 cups seafood stock (or chicken stock)
- 1/2 cup squid ink (nero di seppia)
- 1/2 lb fresh squid, cleaned and sliced into rings
- 2 tbsp butter
- 1/4 cup grated Parmesan cheese
- Salt and pepper to taste
- Fresh parsley, chopped, for garnish

Instructions:

1. Heat olive oil in a large pan over medium heat. Add the chopped onion and cook until soft, about 5 minutes.
2. Stir in the garlic and cook for another minute until fragrant.
3. Add the Arborio rice and toast it for 1-2 minutes until lightly golden.
4. Pour in the white wine and cook until it evaporates.
5. Gradually add the seafood stock, one ladle at a time, stirring continuously and allowing the rice to absorb the liquid before adding more.
6. When the rice is al dente and creamy (about 15-20 minutes), stir in the squid ink and sliced squid. Cook for another 3-4 minutes until the squid is tender.
7. Stir in butter and Parmesan cheese, and season with salt and pepper.
8. Garnish with fresh parsley and serve immediately.

Stuffed Peppers with Rice (Mediterranean)

Ingredients:

- 4 large bell peppers
- 1 cup cooked rice (preferably cold)
- 1/2 lb ground beef or lamb (optional)
- 1 small onion, chopped
- 2 garlic cloves, minced
- 1 tomato, chopped
- 1/4 cup pine nuts (optional)
- 1/4 cup raisins (optional)
- 1 tsp ground cumin
- 1 tsp cinnamon
- 1/4 cup fresh parsley, chopped
- 1/4 cup olive oil
- Salt and pepper to taste
- 1/2 cup tomato sauce

Instructions:

1. Preheat the oven to 375°F (190°C).
2. Cut the tops off the bell peppers and remove the seeds and membranes.
3. In a skillet, heat olive oil over medium heat. Add the chopped onion and garlic, and sauté until soft.
4. Add the ground meat (if using) and cook until browned.
5. Stir in the chopped tomato, pine nuts, raisins, cumin, cinnamon, and cooked rice. Cook for 5 minutes, then stir in the fresh parsley.
6. Season with salt and pepper to taste.
7. Stuff the bell peppers with the rice mixture, pressing down gently to pack them.
8. Place the stuffed peppers in a baking dish. Pour tomato sauce around the peppers and cover with foil.
9. Bake for 30-40 minutes, until the peppers are tender.
10. Serve warm.

Grilled Rice (Japan)

Ingredients:

- 2 cups cooked Japanese short-grain rice (cold)
- 1 tbsp soy sauce
- 1 tbsp sesame oil
- 1 tsp mirin (optional)
- 1/2 tsp toasted sesame seeds
- 1 green onion, finely chopped
- 1 sheet nori (seaweed), shredded (optional)

Instructions:

1. Preheat the grill or grill pan to medium-high heat.
2. In a bowl, mix the cold rice with soy sauce, sesame oil, and mirin.
3. Form the rice into small, compact patties or blocks.
4. Lightly oil the grill grates and place the rice patties on the grill. Grill for 2-3 minutes on each side until they develop crispy grill marks.
5. Remove the grilled rice from the grill and sprinkle with sesame seeds, chopped green onions, and shredded nori.
6. Serve as a side dish or snack.

Red Beans and Rice (USA)

Ingredients:

- 2 cups cooked white rice
- 1 lb dried red beans (or 2 cans red beans, drained and rinsed)
- 1 onion, chopped
- 2 celery stalks, chopped
- 1 green bell pepper, chopped
- 3 garlic cloves, minced
- 2 bay leaves
- 1 tsp thyme
- 1/2 tsp paprika
- 1/4 tsp cayenne pepper (optional, for spice)
- 4 cups water or vegetable broth
- 2 tbsp vegetable oil
- Salt and pepper to taste
- Cooked sausage or ham (optional)

Instructions:

1. In a large pot, heat oil over medium heat. Add the onion, celery, and bell pepper, and sauté until softened, about 5 minutes.
2. Add the garlic, bay leaves, thyme, paprika, and cayenne pepper (if using). Cook for another minute until fragrant.
3. Stir in the red beans and water (or broth). Bring to a boil, then reduce to a simmer.
4. Simmer uncovered for 1-1.5 hours, or until the beans are tender. If using canned beans, reduce the cooking time.
5. Season with salt and pepper to taste.
6. Serve the beans over the cooked rice, and add cooked sausage or ham if desired.

Roasted Rice (Thailand)

Ingredients:

- 1 cup jasmine rice
- 1 tbsp vegetable oil
- 1/2 cup coconut milk
- 1/2 tsp salt
- 1 tbsp toasted sesame seeds (optional)

Instructions:

1. Rinse the rice under cold water until the water runs clear.
2. Heat oil in a dry skillet over medium heat. Add the rinsed rice and cook, stirring constantly, for 5-7 minutes, until the rice turns golden brown.
3. Stir in coconut milk and salt, and bring the mixture to a simmer.
4. Cover and cook on low heat for 15-20 minutes, or until the rice is tender and the liquid is absorbed.
5. Garnish with toasted sesame seeds if desired, and serve warm.

Chahan (Japan)

Ingredients:

- 2 cups cold cooked rice (preferably day-old)
- 2 tbsp vegetable oil
- 1 onion, chopped
- 1/2 cup cooked chicken or shrimp (optional)
- 2 eggs, beaten
- 1/2 cup peas and carrots (frozen or fresh)
- 2 tbsp soy sauce
- 1 tsp sesame oil
- Green onions, chopped, for garnish

Instructions:

1. Heat vegetable oil in a large pan or wok over medium-high heat. Add the chopped onion and cook until soft, about 3-4 minutes.
2. Stir in the cooked chicken or shrimp (if using) and cook for another 2-3 minutes.
3. Push the ingredients to the side of the pan and pour in the beaten eggs. Scramble until cooked through.
4. Add the cold rice, peas, and carrots, and stir-fry for 5-7 minutes until everything is heated through.
5. Stir in the soy sauce and sesame oil, and cook for an additional 2 minutes.
6. Garnish with chopped green onions and serve.

Leblebi Pilavi (Turkey)

Ingredients:

- 1 cup long-grain rice
- 1/4 cup chickpeas (canned or cooked)
- 2 tbsp olive oil
- 1 onion, chopped
- 2 garlic cloves, minced
- 1 tsp cumin
- 1 tsp paprika
- 2 cups vegetable or chicken stock
- Salt and pepper to taste
- Fresh parsley, chopped, for garnish

Instructions:

1. In a large saucepan, heat olive oil over medium heat. Add the chopped onion and garlic, and sauté until soft and golden.
2. Stir in the cumin and paprika, cooking for another minute to release the aromas.
3. Add the rice and chickpeas, stirring to coat them in the spices.
4. Pour in the stock, bring to a boil, then reduce to low heat. Cover and simmer for 15-20 minutes, or until the rice is cooked and the liquid is absorbed.
5. Season with salt and pepper to taste.
6. Garnish with fresh parsley and serve.

Rice with Beans (Brazil)

Ingredients:

- 2 cups cooked white rice
- 1 cup cooked black beans (or canned, drained and rinsed)
- 2 tbsp olive oil
- 1 onion, chopped
- 2 garlic cloves, minced
- 1/4 tsp cumin
- 1/4 tsp paprika
- 1/4 tsp black pepper
- 1/4 cup fresh cilantro, chopped
- 1/4 cup grated coconut (optional)

Instructions:

1. In a large skillet, heat olive oil over medium heat. Add the chopped onion and garlic, and sauté until softened, about 5 minutes.
2. Stir in the cumin, paprika, and black pepper, cooking for another minute.
3. Add the cooked beans and rice, and mix well. Cook for 5-7 minutes until everything is heated through.
4. Stir in the fresh cilantro and grated coconut, if using.
5. Season with additional salt and pepper to taste, and serve warm.

Koshari (Egypt)

Ingredients:

- 1 cup rice
- 1 cup lentils (brown or black)
- 1 cup elbow macaroni or spaghetti, broken into small pieces
- 1 large onion, chopped
- 4 garlic cloves, minced
- 1 can (14 oz) crushed tomatoes
- 1 tbsp ground cumin
- 1 tbsp ground coriander
- 1 tbsp ground cinnamon
- 1/2 tsp ground allspice
- 2 tbsp vinegar
- 2 tbsp olive oil
- Salt and pepper to taste
- Fresh parsley, chopped, for garnish

Instructions:

1. Cook the rice, lentils, and macaroni separately according to their package instructions.
2. In a large skillet, heat the olive oil and sauté the chopped onion until golden brown and crispy. Remove and set aside for garnish.
3. In the same skillet, sauté the minced garlic until fragrant. Add the crushed tomatoes, cumin, coriander, cinnamon, allspice, and vinegar. Stir and cook for about 10 minutes to thicken the sauce. Season with salt and pepper.
4. To assemble, layer the rice, lentils, and macaroni on a serving platter. Pour the tomato sauce over the top.
5. Garnish with crispy onions and fresh parsley. Serve warm.

Lentejas con Arroz (Spain)

Ingredients:

- 1 cup rice
- 1 1/2 cups lentils (green or brown)
- 1 onion, chopped
- 2 garlic cloves, minced
- 1 carrot, chopped
- 1 bell pepper, chopped
- 1 can (14 oz) diced tomatoes
- 1 tbsp paprika
- 1 tsp ground cumin
- 1/2 tsp ground turmeric
- 4 cups vegetable broth or water
- 2 tbsp olive oil
- Salt and pepper to taste
- Fresh parsley, chopped, for garnish

Instructions:

1. Heat olive oil in a large pot and sauté the onion, garlic, carrot, and bell pepper until softened, about 5 minutes.
2. Add the paprika, cumin, turmeric, and diced tomatoes, and cook for another 3 minutes.
3. Stir in the lentils and vegetable broth, bringing to a boil. Reduce to a simmer and cook for about 20 minutes, until lentils are tender.
4. Add the rice and cook for another 10-15 minutes until the rice is fully cooked and the liquid has absorbed. If necessary, add more broth or water.
5. Season with salt and pepper, garnish with fresh parsley, and serve.

Aborrajados Rice (Colombia)

Ingredients:

- 1 cup cooked rice (preferably cold)
- 1/2 lb pork (chopped into small pieces) or chicken
- 1 onion, chopped
- 2 garlic cloves, minced
- 1 tomato, chopped
- 1/2 tsp cumin
- 1/2 tsp paprika
- 1/4 tsp cayenne pepper (optional)
- 1 tbsp vegetable oil
- 1/4 cup chopped cilantro
- Salt and pepper to taste
- 1/2 cup grated cheese (optional)

Instructions:

1. In a large skillet, heat vegetable oil and sauté the chopped onion and garlic until fragrant.
2. Add the chopped pork or chicken, cumin, paprika, and cayenne pepper. Cook until the meat is browned and cooked through.
3. Stir in the chopped tomato and cook for 3-4 minutes until softened.
4. Add the cooked rice to the skillet and mix well. Stir in chopped cilantro and grated cheese if using.
5. Season with salt and pepper to taste and serve warm.

Spicy Rice with Chicken (Mexico)

Ingredients:

- 2 cups rice
- 2 chicken breasts or thighs, cooked and shredded
- 1 onion, chopped
- 2 garlic cloves, minced
- 1 can (14 oz) diced tomatoes with green chilies
- 1/2 cup chicken broth
- 1 tbsp chili powder
- 1 tsp ground cumin
- 1/2 tsp smoked paprika
- 1 tbsp vegetable oil
- 1/2 cup frozen peas (optional)
- Salt and pepper to taste
- Fresh cilantro, chopped, for garnish

Instructions:

1. Heat vegetable oil in a large skillet. Add the chopped onion and garlic, cooking until softened, about 5 minutes.
2. Add the shredded chicken, chili powder, cumin, and paprika. Stir and cook for 2-3 minutes.
3. Stir in the diced tomatoes with green chilies and chicken broth, and bring to a simmer.
4. Add the rice and frozen peas, if using, and mix well. Cover and cook for about 15-20 minutes until the rice is tender and has absorbed the liquid.
5. Season with salt and pepper, garnish with fresh cilantro, and serve.

Stuffed Grape Leaves with Rice (Middle East)

Ingredients:

- 1 jar grape leaves, drained and rinsed
- 1 cup rice
- 1 onion, chopped
- 2 garlic cloves, minced
- 1 tomato, chopped
- 1/4 cup pine nuts (optional)
- 1/4 cup raisins (optional)
- 2 tbsp olive oil
- 1/2 tsp cinnamon
- 1/2 tsp allspice
- 1/4 tsp cumin
- 1/2 cup fresh lemon juice
- Salt and pepper to taste

Instructions:

1. In a skillet, heat olive oil and sauté the onion and garlic until softened.
2. Stir in the rice, cinnamon, allspice, and cumin, and cook for 2-3 minutes.
3. Add the chopped tomato, pine nuts, raisins (if using), and salt and pepper. Stir and cook for another 5 minutes.
4. Place a grape leaf on a flat surface, with the vein side up. Place a spoonful of the rice mixture at the base of the leaf and roll it up tightly, folding in the sides.
5. Repeat with the remaining grape leaves and rice mixture.
6. Arrange the stuffed grape leaves in a large pot, and cover with water and lemon juice. Simmer for 45 minutes, adding more water as needed, until the rice is tender.
7. Serve warm.

Sticky Rice with Pork (Laos)

Ingredients:

- 2 cups sticky rice
- 1/2 lb ground pork
- 1 onion, chopped
- 2 garlic cloves, minced
- 2 tbsp fish sauce
- 1 tbsp soy sauce
- 1 tbsp sugar
- 1/2 tsp ground black pepper
- 1 tbsp vegetable oil
- Fresh cilantro for garnish

Instructions:

1. Rinse the sticky rice and soak it in water for at least 2 hours, or overnight. Steam the rice in a bamboo or metal steamer for 30-40 minutes, until tender.
2. In a skillet, heat vegetable oil over medium heat. Add the onion and garlic, and sauté until softened.
3. Stir in the ground pork and cook until browned.
4. Add the fish sauce, soy sauce, sugar, and black pepper, and cook for another 5-7 minutes, until the flavors are well combined.
5. Serve the pork mixture on top of the sticky rice, garnished with fresh cilantro.

Grits and Rice (USA)

Ingredients:

- 1 cup rice
- 1 cup grits
- 4 cups water or broth
- 2 tbsp butter
- 1/2 cup grated cheddar cheese (optional)
- Salt and pepper to taste

Instructions:

1. Cook the rice according to package instructions.
2. In a separate pot, bring water or broth to a boil. Stir in the grits and reduce the heat to low. Simmer for about 15 minutes, stirring occasionally.
3. Stir in butter, grated cheese (if using), and salt and pepper to taste.
4. Serve the grits alongside the cooked rice, or mix them together.

Savory Rice with Pork (Latin America)

Ingredients:

- 2 cups rice
- 1 lb pork (chopped into small pieces)
- 1 onion, chopped
- 2 garlic cloves, minced
- 1 bell pepper, chopped
- 1 can (14 oz) diced tomatoes
- 1 tsp cumin
- 1 tsp oregano
- 1/2 tsp paprika
- 4 cups chicken broth
- 2 tbsp olive oil
- Salt and pepper to taste
- Fresh cilantro for garnish

Instructions:

1. Heat olive oil in a large skillet. Add the chopped onion, garlic, and bell pepper, cooking until softened, about 5 minutes.
2. Add the chopped pork and cook until browned, about 7 minutes.
3. Stir in the cumin, oregano, paprika, and diced tomatoes. Cook for 3-4 minutes to combine the flavors.
4. Add the rice and chicken broth, bring to a boil, then reduce to low heat. Cover and cook for about 20 minutes, or until the rice is tender and the liquid is absorbed.
5. Season with salt and pepper to taste, garnish with fresh cilantro, and serve.

www.ingramcontent.com/pod-product-compliance
Lightning Source LLC
LaVergne TN
LVHW061955070526
838199LV00060B/4129